Claim Your Aim:
Exodus of a Closed-Mind

RealityPhorism Sages Vol.1

MR. BIGMANN Grier

Claim Your Aim: Exodus of a Closed-Mind Vol.1

Copyright © 2017 MR. BIGMANN Grier.

All rights reserved. Printed in the United States of America. No part of this book may be reproduced or transmitted in any form or by any means, electronic or mechanical- including storage and retrieval system without permission from the publisher- Grier Media Group.

Mr.bigmann@griermediagroup.com

Facebook: Grier Media Group / MrBigmann Grier

Instagram: mr.bigmann_grier

Twitter: @GrierMediaGroup

ISBN-10: 0-9983343-0-8

ISBN-13: 978-0-9983343-0-1

Library of Congress Control Number: 2017902728

Grier Media Group, Macon, GA

Dedicated to those willing to free a Closed-Mind.

CONTENTS

About the Author

RealityPhorism Sages defined

Chapter 1 Recognize who you were born to be *1*

Chapter 2 Connect with your inner self *5*

Chapter 3 Employ educated morals *14*

Chapter 4 Positive Thinking *23*

Chapter 5 Change your mindset *29*

Chapter 6 Educate yourself *47*

Chapter 7 Awareness *55*

Chapter 8 Positive approach to life *66*

Chapter 9 Prosperous life *84*

Chapter 10 Winning! *92*

Author Remarks *97*

ABOUT THE AUTHOR

While experiencing adversity, MR. BIGMANN Grier initiated an open mind. Recognizing that ideas become your reality, he exited a negative closed mind by employing open minded virtues and values, awakening himself to the divinity of his inner self. As an inspirational Reality Poet, MR. BIGMANN Grier encourages an intentional discovery of one's ever-evolving self as he offers inspirational RealityPhorism sages to aid in the exodus of a closed-mind.

"I am MR. BIGMANN Grier whom experienced an exodus of a closed-mind! By acquiring an aspiring positive mindset, I defeated the pain of a negative mind. If you are living with a closed-mind, I can discern and identify with your past and present. For I am you and you are me. Do not allow your life to be contaminated or stagnant. Open your mind with awareness and optimism. Life will positively incline for you. In the streets, stray bullets don't miss…within the world, closed-minds won't succeed far in life!"

–MR. BIGMANN Grier

RealityPhorism Sages:
Sayings of wise, inspirational principles and advice for enduring life.

CHAPTER 1
RECOGNIZE WHO YOU WERE BORN TO BE

There are two types of people in the world... closed-minded people that go with the tide and open-minded people whose grand visions become a living reality.

Which one are you?

Claiming your aim will provide your truth!

You are Success

From exiting the aspirant seed of a man to entering the heavenly womb of a woman, you came to succeed the day you were birthed into the world. Aspiring is your life's motive. Let not negativity move you. Allow positivity to motivate your claim, for your life will continue to successfully aim!

RealityPhorism Sages Volume 1
MR. BIGMANN Grier

You are Success

From exiting as the successive progeny of a man and entering into the procuring womb of a woman; you have been a winner. A winner from the day you were conceived and not just birthed into the world. You are a success and can maintain your life as so, just as the sun maintains a successful radiant glow.

RealityPhorism Sages Volume 1
MR. BIGMANN Grier

You are who you are…regardless of being misunderstood by others of who you truly are.

You are you- forever be true to you!

Recognize who you were born to be…

I am _____

I am _____

I am _____

I am _____

CHAPTER 2
CONNECT WITH YOUR INNER SELF

He who carries hatred with no understanding of its root and with no reason, holds hate for themselves. Detach yourself from any hate you claim.

Aim to claim love in all!

RealityPhorism Sages Volume 1
MR. BIGMANN Grier

Your shadow follows your every move. You are capable to look within yourself and allow your inner light to guide you as you excel.

RealityPhorism Sages Volume 1
MR. BIGMANN Grier

To breathe is to be strong. To live is to have strength.

RealityPhorism Sages Volume 1
MR. BIGMANN Grier

A weak mind encourages a closed- mind. Strong minds inspire an open-mind. Be strong in your aim!

Faith cannot live within a closed-mind. Keep your faith alive with a broad-mind.

RealityPhorism Sages Volume 1
MR. BIGMANN Grier

Life does not exist within mankind's view of aging. Age is solely a number. Age does not determine the fate of your life. You are only as young as your mind.

RealityPhorism Sages Volume 1
MR. BIGMANN Grier

Have will instead of making a wish. For your will power will fulfill fate.

RealityPhorism Sages Volume 1
MR. BIGMANN Grier

While living in the web of a closed-mind, life will never open up to the bliss of your internal self.

You must award your life with expectancy. Whatsoever you expect life to give you- you will be given. Faith acquires your expectations.

Connect with your inner self…

I have faith in _____

I have faith in _____

I have faith in _____

I have faith in _____

CHAPTER 3
EMPLOY EDUCATED MORALS

He who can recognize his needs and wants will be able to obtain those desires. Claim your aim without employing criminal actions in order to possess your wants and fulfill your needs. Aspire to conduct yourself within educated morals.

RealityPhorism Sages Volume 1
MR. BIGMANN Grier

A liar is the twin brother to fake "kicking-it".

RealityPhorism Sages Volume 1
MR. BIGMANN Grier

Transpire so one will feel your worthy effort. Wholeheartedly, employ righteousness aiming towards an open-mind.

RealityPhorism Sages Volume 1
MR. BIGMANN Grier

Evil within the eyes of man is often hard to see. However, evil will reveal evil indeed. Once you become aware it is best to turn away before the evil captivates you. For if you don't, you may have sealed your fate.

Claiming your dignity will open doors for aimed morality.

RealityPhorism Sages Volume 1
MR. BIGMANN Grier

He who lacks self-respect will not respect others. Do not allow disrespect to impede on self-esteem.

Lies are testimonies of deceitfulness. Live in truth.

RealityPhorism Sages Volume 1
MR. BIGMANN Grier

Discrimination is an evil of prejudice. Both are a pestilence to the livelihood of humanity. With a zeal, prejudice has lashed races, cultures, genders and faiths with the realities of discrimination. With the historicity of discrimination, love has become rare within a closed-mind.

To be righteous in spirit, you must be positive at heart.

Employ educated morals…

I will be _____

I will be _____

I will be _____

I will be _____

CHAPTER 4
POSITIVE THINKING

My Open Mind

As I lay back relaxing,

I've come in contact with my deepest open-mind,

A broad mind of great depth, never heights incline

I demand no sip of wine to define.

My purpose I've come to find,

With an open-ended part of my mind-

My open-mind!

The mind's eye that helps me overcome,

All the destruction my eyes have witnessed,

From undergoing as a ghetto boy,

Into my grown man life line,

Being poverty stricken and forced to reflect,

I still can't neglect- my open-mind!

RealityPhorism Sages Volume 1
MR. BIGMANN Grier

What do you see when you…

When you get lost,

Or dwell deep within your open-mind?

I foresee visions that are one of a kind.

Who would consider that a Gangstermen,

Would dwell within the depths of an open-mind.

Due to my past perceptions being closed-minded,

I once lived within the darkest space.

Don't take MR. BIGMANN Grier for granted,

Be aware for my claim is in victories aim.

I claim faith to the depth of my open-mind!

Embrace yourself, apply an open-mind for yourself.

Direct your mind towards your

Deepest reality with an open-mind.

RealityPhorism Sages Volume 1
MR. BIGMANN Grier

Fear of criticism is not an asset to your success.

Closed-minds harvest bad decisions. Open-minds sow good decisions.

RealityPhorism Sages Volume 1
MR. BIGMANN Grier

It takes only one good idea to surpass, to bring fruition to another great idea.

An attentive locus thought will move you without error.

Positive Thinking…

I aim to be _____

I aim to be _____

I aim to be _____

I aim to be _____

CHAPTER 5
CHANGE YOUR MINDSET

Optimism with an open mind

Employ your open-mind thinking beyond pessimism in your life. Think positively before you exert negativity. Think positive before acting out in an enraged manner. Think positive, diverting any negative thoughts. Think positive, moving your closed-mind beyond distress. Think positive, exercising optimism. Think positive!

Explore happiness with an open-mind. Think more, create more, and smile more. A positive mindset can will take your life to never heights. Think positively knowing that you solely control your mind. Think positively and explore blissful thoughts of a peaceful, positive mind. You can put down a harming gun and make claim to open-minded weaponry. Your thoughts will lead you from a closed-minded demise to an optimistic, successful aim.

Life is set to be lived with joy, so enjoy your life by living positively. Feed your life with positive fruit, think positively and discover yourself. What you positively conceive with an open mind can birth happiness. With an open-mind billions of ideas can come to fruition, you can invent a new world. The key is to claim an optimistic, positive mind. Exodus that closed-mind!

*Positive thoughts destroy negative perceptions and diverts negative actions to positive activity.

Think positive!

RealityPhorism Sages Volume 1
MR. BIGMANN Grier

Open your closed-mind to the facts of life. Create an open-faced reality.

ReralityPhorism Sages Volume 1
MR. BIGMANN Grier

Pay attention to what you say…your words today can bring tomorrow's tragedies your way. Think before you speak!

RealityPhorism Sages Volume 1
MR. BIGMANN Grier

You will only go as far as your thoughts take you. Think beyond years, think beyond decades, and think centuries ahead. Think deeply, think infinitely.

RealityPhorism Sages Volume 1
MR. BIGMANN Grier

You will receive the greatest victories, being open-mindedly triumphant.

Starve your mind of negativity. Feed your mind with positivity.

Your ambition to succeed actuates the energy needed to proceed. Progress, aspiring with an open-mind.

Employing an open-mind with positive tenacity will reward your life with favor.

RealityPhorism Sages Volume 1
MR. BIGMANN Grier

Being thoughtless will bring about your demise. One who will not think will not prosper. Aim feeling your claim!

RealityPhorism Sages Volume 1
MR. BIGMANN Grier

Envision your future supports the shaping of your present.

RealityPhorism Sages Volume 1
MR. BIGMANN Grier

Exerting free will gives you infinite creativity.

Always be prepared to improvise through adversity or in abundance. Your advantages come from your aims.

Creative thinking motivates creativity. Creativity makes you an extraordinary creator.

RealityPhorism Sages Volume 1
MR. BIGMANN Grier

Believe not with your ears only, for you are subject to closed-mindedly deceived. Believe with vision and an open-mind, for you will not only receive- you will achieve.

The mind is the strongest magnetic force in the world. What you claim influences your life's existence. Aim open-mindedly and neglect a closed-mind.

RealityPhorism Sages Volume 1
MR. BIGMANN Grier

Self-realization, self-respect, self-confidence and self-control equals self-fulfillment!

Fulfill your self-aspirations!

RealityPhorism Sages Volume 1
MR. BIGMANN Grier

You will only become who you've set out to be.

You will solely speak that which your heart feels.

Whether it's malicious deception or an intentional,

Joyous love inception.

Many live freely with thoughtless emotions.

The passion of emotions can be maintained.

Your feelings devote your motive to arouse,

From the body of your thoughts, your mind's eye.

During moments of anger, love, hate,

Sex, laughter and even thinking,

You can never escape the true feelings of you.

Even when telling a lie,

Your emotions will reveal your truth.

All are emotions that can be aroused from

The depth of your heart.

You will only become who you've set out to be.

CHAPTER 6
EDUCATE YOURSELF

A Great Poet said…

"Use your brain, use your brain!"

-Tupac Shakur, Makaveli 1996

Every day you are a student in the class of life. Whether passing or failing in life, that which you accomplish will manifest. Grade your life according to your aim. Whatever you claim will determine your aim. You are an A student in life when your aim becomes victorious.

RealityPhorism Sages Volume 1
MR. BIGMANN Grier

You are not in control of your life if you cannot control your mind.

RealityPhorism Sages Volume 1
MR. BIGMANN Grier

Knowledge is power…

Use knowledge to intelligently direct your life.

Discover the greatest destination in the world. Explore the nation of your imagination. For we all have access to this suitable resort!

RealityPhorism Sages Volume 1
MR. BIGMANN Grier

A wise gem is not afraid to be advised. Only a fool will admire deterring advice.

Illiteracy breeds ignorance. Never reject education. Know-how is how you reap the world!

Be dedicated to being educated!

"They say the way that I was living influenced the youth. Young brothers dropping out of school like it's the thing to do. But I'm a testimony for the youngn's, I try to tell em' they're not listening, the hood is steady taking them under.

-Pookie Loc, American Dream 2001

CHAPTER 7
AWARENESS

Mature Motivation

Think beyond foolish precepts.

You can turn nothing into something.

Have the ambition to overcome a closed-mind,

And succeed with an open-mind.

Not just with the riches of affluence,

But abundance within your life.

Brave hearts feed your mind,

Self-realization is one of a kind.

Mature motivation comes about

From an exodus of a closed-mind.

Claim your aim, exodus a closed-mind.

Envelop free will thoughts for the mind.

You'll sin until you sin not,

RealityPhorism Sages Volume 1
MR. BIGMANN Grier

You don't have to uphold negativity.

It is evident when you perceive what you've got.

You can open up with positivity.

Let your aim soar to never heights.

If you desire to know the real in you,

Mature motivation within your life,

Will innovate that light.

Constructive criticism can be your truest friend.

Be aware of feminine power, masculinity can suffer defeat through sexuality.

Trust is not built, it exists in truth. Betrayal is what is built from untrustworthiness.

RealityPhorism Sages Volume 1
MR. BIGMANN Grier

You can recognize the real in someone when you can see the truth in someone.

Giving is a passion of sacrifice, and sacrifice comes as an affection of giving. Both, open-heartedly omit love.

RealityPhorism Sages Volume 1
MR. BIGMANN Grier

A man's heart is the most powerful thing he can submit to a woman. A woman's emotions are the most powerful thing she can submit to a man.

RealityPhorism Sages Volume 1
MR. BIGMANN Grier

You must have a motive and objective in order to fulfill your purpose.

RealityPhorism Sages Volume 1
MR. BIGMANN Grier

"Their underestimation is your best preparation!"

-Sonny Campbell, 2017

There are many closed-minded people in the world. You must not allow closed-minded individuals to affect your choices. Refrain from allowing them to give you ill advice. Doing so could be detrimental to your life's fate. Open your mind to making your own choices. You are the one who will experience your own life. Responsibly make your own decisions with an open-mind. Claim your aim as you are the benefactor of your life.

Awareness…

I choose to _____

I choose to_____

I choose to _____

I choose to _____

CHAPTER 8
POSITIVE APPROACH TO LIFE

We graze upon the field of life as one great herd. Yet, we are individuals on which life can prey. You must exodus a closed-mind for we live in a new age; an era of open door opportunities to be upon the highest class.

RealityPhorism Sages Volume 1
MR. BIGMANN Grier

Game is only a game when you have mastered the play. When the game controls you- then you are being played.

RealityPhorism Sages Volume 1
MR. BIGMANN Grier

When you fertilize the cause in your life you will birth an effect! Claim an effective feeling.

RealityPhorism Sages Volume 1
MR. BIGMANN Grier

Excuses are the sisters to procrastination.

Time + Space + Circumstance = Opportunity to grow

RealityPhorism Sages Volume 1
MR. BIGMANN Grier

Drive towards your goals with nothing to lose, but with the world to gain.

Your past is only a piece of the mold that shapes your future life. Experiences help construct your fate.

One without enthusiasm to live has no purpose.

Action is the perseverance you employ in order to prevail in life. Take massive action!

Attention to stress is bowing to life's misery.
Preserve calmness and endure a positive life.

RealityPhorism Sages Volume 1
MR. BIGMANN Grier

Perceive with an open-mind before you act. Your next step will come from a progressive approach.

Any risk is a gamble. Be conversant with risk management.

RealityPhorism Sages Volume 1
MR. BIGMANN Grier

A life without direction is subject to wreck. The nervous hand reflects an off course life.

RealityPhorism Sages Volume 1
MR. BIGMANN Grier

Walk knowing where you are going. Today's moves shape your life in the future. Tomorrow is today so aim to accomplish every day.

RealityPhorism Sages Volume 1
MR. BIGMANN Grier

Decide who you are through your aims. Your arms reach is not as far as you can go. One who lives as if there is no tomorrow may not be able to see as far. Pace yourself. Give attention to your decisions. Decide who you are through your aim. You can go as far as you aim in life.

RealityPhorism Sages Volume 1
MR. BIGMANN Grier

Living life void of high spirits is like a having a heart without a beat… detrimental!

Nothing will come to you until surely you work persistently. Your patience is within the perseverance of your effort to aim.

RealityPhorism Sages Volume 1
MR. BIGMANN Grier

To die is to have had life. Fulfill all your life's aspiration before you die. Fail to let your aim be a quicker demise. In the spirit of aiming, live to rise!

Positive approach to life…

I aspire to_____

I aspire to _____

I aspire to _____

I aspire to _____

CHAPTER 9
PROSPEROUS LIFE

The value of money can be detrimental to one's value of life. Therefore, making life priceless!

The seed of monetary success is claiming an aim in financially investing your money. Financial literacy waters that seed successfully.

Money is formulated from ideas and knowledge.

RealityPhorism Sages Volume 1
MR. BIGMANN Grier

You can beget money from your ideas and ideas others lose to you.

The hustle towards prosperity expands, it never stops.

RealityPhorism Sages Volume 1
MR. BIGMANN Grier

Money is power… know how to direct money to work for you.

RealityPhorism Sages Volume 1
MR. BIGMANN Grier

When money is entrusted it can return with spite. Give with an open heart and it will be paid back with love.

Success is a seed in the mind awaiting fresh water thoughts. Thinking with an open-mind exerts triumphant water.

Prosperous life…

I plan to _____

I plan to _____

I plan to _____

I plan to _____

CHAPTER 10
WINNING!

Think in advance towards your aim. Thank yourself in advance for claiming your aim!

RealityPhorism Sages Volume 1
MR. BIGMANN Grier

One who perseveres through thought, outthinks the rest.

Failure can drive you to excel. Failing can cultivate excellence!

RealityPhorism Sages Volume 1
MR. BIGMANN Grier

Failure is not an end. To fail can be to prevail.

Love yourself! Award your life with love and in return it will love you back even stronger.

Winning! ...

I love my _____

I love my _____

I love my _____

I love my _____

RealityPhorism Sages Volume 1
MR. BIGMANN Grier

Claim Your Aim

Exodus of a closed-mind is designed to open minds.

No worries disturb his broad-mind.

He's concerned about the lives not aiming to live,

From the mantic reality-truth of an exodus

From a closed-mind to live.

Life is wealth!

The more you breathe,

Your life will opulently earn!

He's claiming an aim, inspiring

Closed-minds to think, apply and learn.

Prosperity isn't precisely a sum in his pockets;

It is the growth of an open mind,

Abundance he yearns.

He dares not encourage narrow mindedness.

The reality he condones will not mindfully condemn.

RealityPhorism Sages Volume 1
MR. BIGMANN Grier

It is evident your mind will be opened,

To open doors for your claimed satisfaction.

Claiming your aim is all about inspiring action.

RealityPhorism Sages Volume 1
MR. BIGMANN Grier

"I was once described as a man who can sell anyone a dream. I hope the dream you just experienced keeps your mind forever open. Claim your aim!"

-MR. BIGMANN Grier

RealityPhorism Sages Volume 1
MR. BIGMANN Grier

Grier Media Group Presents...

Manning Up:

PoesyEssays of Women's Interest

By: MR. BIGMANN Grier

Available in E-book and Paperback on Amazon.com & Createspace.com

Coming Soon...

Reality Poetry-

Ark of Inspirational Wisdom

By: MR. BIGMANN Grier

www.ingramcontent.com/pod-product-compliance
Lightning Source LLC
Chambersburg PA
CBHW031157160426
43193CB00008B/405